Welcome to t

Kia ora, mate! You've just stumbled upon the ultimate guide to sounding like a true Kiwi—without having to worry about learning to pronounce "Wellington" properly (because, let's be real, it's "Welly," isn't it?). Whether you're just visiting, or you're looking to fit in with the locals, this book will have you saying "sweet as" in no time.

In New Zealand, we don't just "talk," we have a whole new language—and no, it's not just sheep-related (though, let's be honest, they might be listening). From the "jandals" on your feet to the "chur" you say when something's awesome, this book's got all the slang you'll need to impress your mates, avoid looking like a tourist, or just have a laugh when things go "taka."

So, grab your "fush and chups" (that's fish and chips, if you didn't know), put your best "stoked" face on, and dive in—you'll soon be talking like you've been living in Aotearoa for years. Just don't ask us to explain "bro"—it's a word that means everything and nothing, and we're not sure even we understand it completely!

TABLE OF CONTENT

Where is your next travel ?

SCAN THE QR

Get the Slang Dictionary Collection

Slang Dictionaries Availables:

-French   -Italian
-Mexican   -Colombian
-German   -Many More...

A

1. **A bit of a dag**
   Meaning: A funny or quirky person.
   Example: "He's a bit of a dag, always cracking jokes."
   Translation: "He's quite a character, always making jokes."

2. **Aotearoa**
   Meaning: Māori name for New Zealand, meaning "Land of the Long White Cloud."
   Example: "Welcome to Aotearoa, bro!"
   Translation: "Welcome to New Zealand, mate!"

3. **Arvo**
   Meaning: Afternoon.
   Example: "Let's meet up this arvo for a coffee."
   Translation: "Let's meet this afternoon for a coffee."

4. **Away with the fairies**
   Meaning: Daydreaming or not paying attention.
   Example: "Oi, stop being away with the fairies and focus!"
   Translation: "Hey, stop daydreaming and pay attention!"

5. **Awesome**
   Meaning: Great, excellent.
   Example: "That surf session was awesome!"
   Translation: "That surfing session was fantastic!"

6. **As** (used as a suffix for emphasis)
   Meaning: Extremely.
   Example: "It's cold as today."
   Translation: "It's extremely cold today."

7. **A bit naff**
   Meaning: Lame or uncool.
   Example: "That movie was a bit naff, eh?"
   Translation: "That movie was kind of lame, right?"

8. **Ace**
   Meaning: Great, excellent.
   Example: "The concert last night was ace!"
   Translation: "The concert last night was excellent!"

9. **Ankle-biter**
   Meaning: A small child.
   Example: "The ankle-biters are playing in the backyard."
   Translation: "The small children are playing in the backyard."

10. **All good**
    Meaning: No worries; everything is fine.
    Example: "Forgot to text you back, mate." "All good!"
    Translation: "I forgot to text you back, mate." "No worries!"

11. **Aroha**
    Meaning: Māori word for love, compassion.
    Example: "Sending aroha to everyone affected."
    Translation: "Sending love to everyone affected."

12. **As keen as mustard**
    Meaning: Very eager.
    Example: "She was as keen as mustard to get started."
    Translation: "She was very eager to get started."

13. **A bit of alright**
    Meaning: Something or someone attractive.
    Example: "That new car of yours is a bit of alright!"
    Translation: "That new car of yours is pretty nice!"

14. **Aussie**
    Meaning: Australian.
    Example: "We met some Aussies on our trip to Queenstown."
    Translation: "We met some Australians on our trip to Queenstown."

15. **Awks**
    Meaning: Short for awkward.
    Example: "That was awks when he forgot my name!"
    Translation: "That was awkward when he forgot my name!"

16. **Avo**
    Meaning: Avocado.
    Example: "Smash some avo on toast for brekkie."
    Translation: "Put some mashed avocado on toast for breakfast."

17. **A bit iffy**
    Meaning: Uncertain or questionable.
    Example: "The weather looks a bit iffy for the hike."
    Translation: "The weather looks uncertain for the hike."

18. **Aotearoa hard**
    Meaning: Strongly identifies with New Zealand.
    Example: "She's Aotearoa hard, loves the culture and the rugby."

Translation: "She's very Kiwi, loves the culture and rugby."

19. **Amber nectar**

Meaning: Beer.

Example: "Pass me another amber nectar from the chilly bin."

Translation: "Pass me another beer from the cooler."

20. **Away laughing**

Meaning: On the right track or successful.

Example: "Once you get the hang of it, you'll be away laughing."

Translation: "Once you get the hang of it, you'll do well."

B

1. **Bach**
   Meaning: A small holiday home, typically near the beach.
   Example: "We're heading to the bach this weekend."
   Translation: "We're going to the holiday house this weekend."

2. **Back of beyond**
   Meaning: A remote or isolated place.
   Example: "Their farm is out in the back of beyond."
   Translation: "Their farm is in a very remote area."

3. **Bangers**
   Meaning: Sausages.
   Example: "We'll chuck some bangers on the barbie tonight."
   Translation: "We'll grill some sausages on the barbecue tonight."

4. **Barbie**
   Meaning: Barbecue.
   Example: "Let's have a barbie down at the beach."
   Translation: "Let's have a barbecue at the beach."

5. **Beaut**
   Meaning: Wonderful, great.
   Example: "That view from the hill is an absolute beaut!"
   Translation: "That view from the hill is absolutely beautiful!"

6. **Bogan**
   Meaning: Someone with an uncultured or

working-class style, often rural.
Example: "He's such a bogan with his mullet and flannel."
Translation: "He's so uncultured with his mullet and flannel shirt."

7. **Bottle-O**
Meaning: Liquor store.
Example: "I'm heading to the Bottle-O to grab some beers."
Translation: "I'm going to the liquor store to get some beers."

8. **Brekkie**
Meaning: Breakfast.
Example: "We had a massive brekkie of eggs and bacon."
Translation: "We had a big breakfast of eggs and bacon."

9. **Bring a plate**
Meaning: Bring food to share.
Example: "It's a potluck, so don't forget to bring a plate."
Translation: "It's a potluck, so bring some food to share."

10. **Bro**
Meaning: Friend or mate (can also mean brother).
Example: "Cheers, bro, for helping me move."
Translation: "Thanks, mate, for helping me move."

11. **Bugger all**
Meaning: Very little or nothing.
Example: "There's bugger all food left after the party."
Translation: "There's almost no food left after the party."

12. **Bush**
    Meaning: Forested or rural area.
    Example: "We're going hiking in the bush tomorrow."
    Translation: "We're going hiking in the forest tomorrow."

13. **Buzzing**
    Meaning: Excited or happy.
    Example: "I'm buzzing for the game tonight!"
    Translation: "I'm so excited for the game tonight!"

14. **Byo**
    Meaning: Bring your own (often referring to alcohol).
    Example: "The party is BYO, so bring your drinks."
    Translation: "The party is bring your own, so bring your drinks."

15. **Bit of a yarn**
    Meaning: A casual or light-hearted chat.
    Example: "We had a bit of a yarn about the rugby."
    Translation: "We had a casual chat about the rugby."

16. **Bung**
    Meaning: Broken or damaged.
    Example: "My car's all bung after hitting that pothole."
    Translation: "My car's damaged after hitting that pothole."

17. **Bloke**
    Meaning: A man, usually an ordinary guy.
    Example: "He's a good bloke, always willing to lend a hand."

Translation: "He's a good guy, always willing to help."

18. **Buzzy**

    Meaning: Strange or fascinating.
    Example: "That was a buzzy experience at the museum."
    Translation: "That was a fascinating experience at the museum."

19. **Bashed up**

    Meaning: Beaten or damaged.
    Example: "His old car is completely bashed up."
    Translation: "His old car is completely damaged."

20. **Box of birds**

    Meaning: Feeling happy or cheerful.
    Example: "I'm feeling a box of birds this morning!"
    Translation: "I'm feeling cheerful this morning!"

C

1. **Chilly bin**
   Meaning: Cooler or portable icebox.
   Example: "Grab a beer from the chilly bin, mate."
   Translation: "Take a beer from the cooler, mate."

2. **Chocka**
   Meaning: Completely full.
   Example: "The bus was chocka, so I had to wait for the next one."
   Translation: "The bus was completely full, so I had to wait for the next one."

3. **Choice**
   Meaning: Awesome, excellent.
   Example: "That concert was so choice!"
   Translation: "That concert was amazing!"

4. **Carked it**
   Meaning: Died or broken down.
   Example: "The lawnmower carked it halfway through the job."
   Translation: "The lawnmower broke down halfway through the task."

5. **Cheeky**
   Meaning: Playfully rude or mischievous.
   Example: "He gave me a cheeky wink when he passed by."
   Translation: "He playfully winked at me as he walked by."

6. **Cooked**
   Meaning: Exhausted or completely messed up.
   Example: "After the hike, I was absolutely cooked."

14

Translation: "After the hike, I was completely exhausted."

7. **Cruisy**
   Meaning: Relaxed or easy-going.
   Example: "The job was pretty cruisy, no stress at all."
   Translation: "The job was very relaxed, no stress at all."

8. **Cuppa**
   Meaning: A cup of tea.
   Example: "Fancy a cuppa before heading out?"
   Translation: "Would you like a cup of tea before heading out?"

9. **Chur**
   Meaning: Thanks or cool.
   Example: "Chur, bro, for helping me out."
   Translation: "Thanks, mate, for helping me out."

10. **Clapped out**
    Meaning: Worn out or broken down.
    Example: "That old car is clapped out, mate."
    Translation: "That old car is completely worn out."

11. **Crook**
    Meaning: Sick or unwell.
    Example: "I'm feeling crook today, might stay in bed."
    Translation: "I'm feeling sick today, so I might stay in bed."

12. **Cut lunch**
    Meaning: Sandwiches.
    Example: "Grab some cut lunch for the hike tomorrow."
    Translation: "Pack some sandwiches for the hike tomorrow."

13. **Can't be bothered**
    Meaning: Lacking the energy or interest to do something.
    Example: "I can't be bothered cooking tonight, let's get takeaways."
    Translation: "I don't feel like cooking tonight; let's get takeout."
14. **Catch you later**
    Meaning: Goodbye or see you later.
    Example: "I'm off now, catch you later!"
    Translation: "I'm leaving now; see you later!"
15. **Call it a day**
    Meaning: Stop working or doing an activity.
    Example: "We've done enough, let's call it a day."
    Translation: "We've done enough; let's stop for now."
16. **Cuzzie**
    Meaning: Close friend or cousin.
    Example: "How's it going, cuzzie?"
    Translation: "How are you, my friend?"
17. **Chock-full**
    Meaning: Completely full.
    Example: "The chilly bin is chock-full of beers."
    Translation: "The cooler is completely full of beers."
18. **Cold one**
    Meaning: A beer.
    Example: "Let's crack open a cold one."
    Translation: "Let's open a beer."
19. **Cheese cutter**
    Meaning: A flat cap.
    Example: "Grandad always wore a cheese cutter on sunny days."

Translation: "Grandad always wore a flat cap on sunny days."

20. **Caned it**

Meaning: Went fast or excelled.

Example: "He really caned it in the race!"

Translation: "He went really fast in the race!"

D

1. **Dag**
   Meaning: A funny or quirky person.
   Example: "She's such a dag, always cracking us up."
   Translation: "She's so funny, always making us laugh."

2. **Dairy**
   Meaning: A small corner store.
   Example: "I'll grab some milk from the dairy."
   Translation: "I'll get some milk from the convenience store."

3. **Dole**
   Meaning: Unemployment benefits.
   Example: "He's been on the dole since he lost his job."
   Translation: "He's been receiving unemployment benefits since losing his job."

4. **Do a runner**
   Meaning: Leave quickly or escape, often to avoid trouble.
   Example: "He did a runner when the bill came!"
   Translation: "He ran off when the bill arrived!"

5. **Dunny**
   Meaning: Toilet.
   Example: "I need to find a dunny; it's urgent."
   Translation: "I need to find a toilet; it's urgent."

6. **Drongo**
   Meaning: A foolish or silly person.
   Example: "Don't be such a drongo, mate!"
   Translation: "Don't act so foolish, mate!"

7. **Deadset**

   Meaning: Seriously or truly.

   Example: "Deadset, that's the best fish and chips I've had!"

   Translation: "Seriously, that's the best fish and chips I've had!"

8. **Dodgy**

   Meaning: Shady or untrustworthy.

   Example: "That car salesman seems a bit dodgy."

   Translation: "That car salesman seems a bit untrustworthy."

9. **Decked out**

   Meaning: Fully dressed or outfitted.

   Example: "She was decked out in All Blacks gear for the game."

   Translation: "She was fully dressed in All Blacks attire for the game."

10. **Dog's breakfast**

    Meaning: A mess or disaster.

    Example: "This report is a dog's breakfast; we'll need to redo it."

    Translation: "This report is a mess; we'll need to do it again."

11. **Drive you up the wall**

    Meaning: Annoy or frustrate greatly.

    Example: "The noisy neighbors are driving me up the wall."

    Translation: "The noisy neighbors are extremely annoying me."

12. **DIY**

    Meaning: Do It Yourself (often referring to home repairs).

    Example: "I'm tackling a DIY project this weekend."

Translation: "I'm doing a home repair project myself this weekend."

13. **Dished up**
Meaning: Served or presented.
Example: "Mum dished up an amazing roast dinner."
Translation: "Mum served an amazing roast dinner."

14. **Down a treat**
Meaning: Enjoyed thoroughly.
Example: "That pavlova went down a treat at the party."
Translation: "That pavlova was thoroughly enjoyed at the party."

15. **Duck's nuts**
Meaning: The best or perfect thing.
Example: "This new phone is the duck's nuts!"
Translation: "This new phone is amazing!"

16. **Do the hard yards**
Meaning: Put in significant effort or work.
Example: "You've got to do the hard yards if you want results."
Translation: "You need to work hard if you want to succeed."

17. **Dust-up**
Meaning: A fight or argument.
Example: "There was a bit of a dust-up at the pub last night."
Translation: "There was a bit of a fight at the bar last night."

18. **Ditch**
Meaning: To leave or abandon.
Example: "They ditched me at the mall!"
Translation: "They left me at the mall!"

19. **Dropkick**
    Meaning: A useless or foolish person.
    Example: "Don't be such a dropkick and get the job done!"
    Translation: "Don't be so foolish and finish the job!"
20. **Drinkies**
    Meaning: Informal drinks, often alcoholic.
    Example: "We're having drinkies at mine tonight."
    Translation: "We're having drinks at my place tonight."

E

1. **Eke out**
   Meaning: To make something last or stretch.
   Example: "We'll have to eke out this bread until payday."
   Translation: "We'll have to make this bread last until payday."

2. **Eh?**
   Meaning: Added to the end of a sentence for emphasis or agreement, like "right?"
   Example: "That was a great game, eh?"
   Translation: "That was a great game, right?"

3. **Egg**
   Meaning: To encourage someone, often to do something risky.
   Example: "Don't egg him on, he'll actually do it!"
   Translation: "Don't encourage him; he'll actually do it!"

4. **Earful**
   Meaning: A lengthy scolding or reprimand.
   Example: "Mum gave me an earful for coming home late."
   Translation: "Mum scolded me for coming home late."

5. **Elbow grease**
   Meaning: Physical effort.
   Example: "You'll need some elbow grease to scrub that floor."
   Translation: "You'll need physical effort to clean that floor."

6. **End of the line**
   Meaning: The final option or point.

Example: "If this doesn't work, it's the end of the line for the project."
Translation: "If this doesn't work, it's the final option for the project."

7. **Eh bro?**
Meaning: A casual greeting or way to start a conversation with a friend.
Example: "Eh bro, what's the plan for tonight?"
Translation: "Hey man, what's the plan for tonight?"

8. **Eat your hat**
Meaning: An expression to indicate disbelief.
Example: "If they win, I'll eat my hat!"
Translation: "If they win, I'll be shocked!"

9. **Even Stevens**
Meaning: Equal or fair.
Example: "We paid half each, so it's even Stevens."
Translation: "We each paid half, so it's fair."

10. **Esky**
Meaning: A portable cooler for drinks and food.
Example: "Grab the Esky for the picnic."
Translation: "Take the cooler for the picnic."

11. **Earn your stripes**
Meaning: To prove your worth or gain experience.
Example: "He earned his stripes after years of hard work."
Translation: "He proved his worth after years of hard work."

12. **Easy as**
Meaning: Very simple.
Example: "Building this shelf is easy as."

Translation: "Building this shelf is very simple."

13. **Egged out**

Meaning: Overwhelmed or exhausted.

Example: "I was egged out after that all-nighter."

Translation: "I was completely exhausted after staying up all night."

14. **Every man and his dog**

Meaning: A large crowd or everyone.

Example: "Every man and his dog was at the concert."

Translation: "Everyone was at the concert."

15. **Ear to the ground**

Meaning: Staying aware or alert to new information.

Example: "Keep your ear to the ground for job openings."

Translation: "Stay alert for new job opportunities."

16. **Eats**

Meaning: Food, often informal or quick.

Example: "Let's grab some eats before the show."

Translation: "Let's grab some food before the show."

17. **Easy peasy**

Meaning: Very easy or simple.

Example: "Fixing that bike is easy peasy."

Translation: "Fixing that bike is very simple."

18. **Eh what?**

Meaning: A phrase to express surprise or disbelief.

Example: "You're moving to Aussie, eh what?"

Translation: "You're moving to Australia, really?"

19. **Eager beaver**
Meaning: Someone overly enthusiastic.
Example: "The new guy is such an eager beaver."
Translation: "The new guy is very enthusiastic."

20. **Ear-bash**
Meaning: Talk excessively or nag.
Example: "She gave me an ear-bash about cleaning my room."
Translation: "She nagged me a lot about cleaning my room."

F

1. **Faff about**
   Meaning: To waste time or act ineffectively.
   Example: "Stop faffing about and get the job done."
   Translation: "Stop wasting time and finish the task."

2. **Flat out**
   Meaning: Extremely busy or working hard.
   Example: "I've been flat out all week at work."
   Translation: "I've been extremely busy all week at work."

3. **Fizzy drink**
   Meaning: A carbonated soft drink.
   Example: "Grab me a fizzy drink from the fridge."
   Translation: "Get me a soda from the fridge."

4. **Flick**
   Meaning: To send something or get rid of something.
   Example: "I'll flick you an email later."
   Translation: "I'll send you an email later."

5. **Flog**
   Meaning: To sell or steal something.
   Example: "He tried to flog his old bike for a hundred bucks."
   Translation: "He tried to sell his old bike for a hundred dollars."

6. **Frosty**
   Meaning: A cold beer.
   Example: "Let's crack open a frosty after work."

Translation: "Let's open a cold beer after work."

7. **Fit as a fiddle**
   Meaning: Very healthy or in good shape.
   Example: "Grandad's fit as a fiddle for his age."
   Translation: "Grandad is very healthy for his age."

8. **Fizzer**
   Meaning: Something that fails or is disappointing.
   Example: "The fireworks were a real fizzer this year."
   Translation: "The fireworks were really disappointing this year."

9. **Footy**
   Meaning: Rugby or Australian Rules Football.
   Example: "We're off to watch the footy this weekend."
   Translation: "We're going to watch the rugby game this weekend."

10. **Flick the switch**
    Meaning: Change suddenly or start something.
    Example: "It's time to flick the switch and focus."
    Translation: "It's time to change gears and concentrate."

11. **Full-on**
    Meaning: Intense or extreme.
    Example: "That storm last night was full-on!"
    Translation: "That storm last night was really intense!"

12. **Fair go**
    Meaning: A fair chance or opportunity.
    Example: "Everyone deserves a fair go in life."

Translation: "Everyone deserves a fair chance in life."

13. **Fang it**
Meaning: To drive or move quickly.
Example: "Fang it, or we'll be late!"
Translation: "Hurry up, or we'll be late!"

14. **Fend for yourself**
Meaning: Take care of yourself without help.
Example: "When the parents went out, we had to fend for ourselves."
Translation: "When our parents went out, we had to manage on our own."

15. **Flicked off**
Meaning: To get rid of or ignore someone.
Example: "I flicked off the salesperson after they kept calling."
Translation: "I ignored the salesperson after they kept calling."

16. **Fritter away**
Meaning: Waste time or money.
Example: "Don't fritter away your paycheck on junk."
Translation: "Don't waste your paycheck on useless things."

17. **Flash**
Meaning: Fancy or impressive.
Example: "That's a flash car you've got there."
Translation: "That's a fancy car you have there."

18. **Flat tack**
Meaning: At full speed or maximum effort.
Example: "We're going flat tack to meet the deadline."
Translation: "We're working at full speed to meet the deadline."

19. **Freebie**
    Meaning: Something given for free.
    Example: "They gave out freebies at the game."
    Translation: "They handed out free items at the game."
20. **Froth**
    Meaning: To be excited about something.
    Example: "He's frothing over the new All Blacks jersey."
    Translation: "He's really excited about the new All Blacks jersey."

G

1. **G'day**
   Meaning: A casual greeting; short for "Good day."
   Example: "G'day, mate! How's it going?"
   Translation: "Hello, friend! How are you doing?"

2. **Guts for garters**
   Meaning: A playful or serious threat.
   Example: "If you touch my tools again, it's your guts for garters!"
   Translation: "If you touch my tools again, you'll be in big trouble!"

3. **Good as gold**
   Meaning: Excellent or trustworthy.
   Example: "Thanks for fixing the fence, you're good as gold."
   Translation: "Thanks for fixing the fence, you're excellent."

4. **Gone burger**
   Meaning: Finished or over.
   Example: "Once the engine overheated, the car was gone burger."
   Translation: "Once the engine overheated, the car was completely finished."

5. **Give it heaps**
   Meaning: Put in lots of effort or energy.
   Example: "When you're out there on the field, give it heaps!"
   Translation: "When you're out there on the field, put in maximum effort!"

6. **Get amongst it**
   Meaning: Join in or participate enthusiastically.

Example: "The concert's about to start, so get amongst it!"

Translation: "The concert's about to start, so join in and enjoy!"

7. **Grouse**

Meaning: Fantastic or excellent.

Example: "That new café down the road is grouse!"

Translation: "That new café down the road is fantastic!"

8. **Gasbag**

Meaning: Someone who talks a lot.

Example: "She's a bit of a gasbag when she gets going."

Translation: "She talks a lot once she starts."

9. **Good on ya**

Meaning: Well done or good for you.

Example: "You passed your driving test? Good on ya!"

Translation: "You passed your driving test? Well done!"

10. **Grog**

Meaning: Alcoholic drinks.

Example: "We need to pick up some grog for the barbecue."

Translation: "We need to get some alcohol for the barbecue."

11. **Go bush**

Meaning: Retreat to the wilderness or countryside.

Example: "I need a break; I'm going bush for a week."

Translation: "I need a break; I'm heading to the countryside for a week."

12. **Gutful**
Meaning: Had enough of something; annoyed.
Example: "I've had a gutful of your excuses!"
Translation: "I'm fed up with your excuses!"

13. **Gutted**
Meaning: Extremely disappointed.
Example: "I was gutted when we lost the match."
Translation: "I was extremely disappointed when we lost the match."

14. **Get stuck in**
Meaning: Dive into something enthusiastically
Example: "Lunch is ready, so get stuck in!"
Translation: "Lunch is ready, so dig in!"

15. **Give it a whirl**
Meaning: Try something.
Example: "Never tried surfing before? Give it a whirl!"
Translation: "Never tried surfing before? Try it out!"

16. **Go on the piss**
Meaning: Go out drinking.
Example: "We're going on the piss after work."
Translation: "We're going out drinking after work."

17. **Gnarly**
Meaning: Cool or impressive, often in a rugged way.
Example: "That was a gnarly wave you caught!"
Translation: "That was an impressive wave you surfed!"

18. **Give someone a bell**
Meaning: Call someone on the phone.
Example: "I'll give you a bell later tonight."
Translation: "I'll call you later tonight."

19. **Good keen man**
    Meaning: A hardworking, capable person.
    Example: "He's a good keen man, always helping out."
    Translation: "He's a hardworking and dependable person."
20. **Go hard**
    Meaning: Put in maximum effort.
    Example: "If you want to win, you've got to go hard."
    Translation: "If you want to win, you need to give it your all."

H

1. **Hard case**
   Meaning: A funny or quirky person.
   Example: "That guy's a real hard case, always cracking jokes."
   Translation: "That guy is very funny and quirky, always making jokes."

2. **Haka**
   Meaning: A traditional Māori dance or chant, often performed before rugby games.
   Example: "The All Blacks' haka before the game was incredible."
   Translation: "The All Blacks' traditional dance before the game was amazing."

3. **Hard yakka**
   Meaning: Hard work or tough effort.
   Example: "It was hard yakka digging that garden."
   Translation: "It was hard work digging that garden."

4. **Hoon**
   Meaning: A reckless or noisy driver.
   Example: "Some hoon was doing burnouts in the car park."
   Translation: "Some reckless driver was doing stunts in the car park."

5. **Harden up**
   Meaning: Toughen up or stop complaining.
   Example: "Come on, harden up, it's only a bit of rain!"
   Translation: "Come on, toughen up, it's just a little rain!"

6. **Hangry**
   Meaning: Irritable because of hunger.
   Example: "Don't talk to me, I'm hangry and need food."
   Translation: "Don't talk to me; I'm irritable because I'm hungry."

7. **Have a gander**
   Meaning: To take a look at something.
   Example: "Have a gander at this new phone I got."
   Translation: "Take a look at this new phone I bought."

8. **Hassle**
   Meaning: To bother or annoy someone.
   Example: "Stop hassling me about cleaning my room!"
   Translation: "Stop bothering me about cleaning my room!"

9. **Hot as**
   Meaning: Extremely attractive or appealing.
   Example: "That car is hot as, mate!"
   Translation: "That car is incredibly appealing, friend!"

10. **Half-pie**
    Meaning: Half-done or mediocre.
    Example: "This job is only half-pie finished."
    Translation: "This job is only half-done."

11. **Heaps**
    Meaning: A lot or many.
    Example: "There were heaps of people at the festival."
    Translation: "There were a lot of people at the festival."

12. **Hack it**
    Meaning: Handle or cope with something.

Example: "If you can't hack it, maybe this job isn't for you."
Translation: "If you can't handle it, maybe this job isn't suitable for you."

13. **Hit the hay**
Meaning: Go to bed or sleep.
Example: "I'm knackered, time to hit the hay."
Translation: "I'm exhausted; it's time to go to sleep."

14. **Hissy fit**
Meaning: A tantrum or outburst.
Example: "She threw a hissy fit when they ran out of coffee."
Translation: "She had a tantrum when they ran out of coffee."

15. **Hot under the collar**
Meaning: Angry or annoyed.
Example: "He got hot under the collar when he lost the game."
Translation: "He got annoyed when he lost the game."

16. **Hoopla**
Meaning: Fuss or excitement.
Example: "What's all the hoopla about this new phone?"
Translation: "What's all the excitement about this new phone?"

17. **Hitch a ride**
Meaning: To get a lift with someone.
Example: "I'll hitch a ride with you to the beach."
Translation: "I'll get a lift with you to the beach."

18. **Hard out**
Meaning: Definitely or for sure.

Example: "You're coming to the party, hard out!"

Translation: "You're definitely coming to the party!"

19. **Hottie**

Meaning: A hot water bottle or an attractive person.

Example: "I need my hottie; it's freezing tonight."

Translation: "I need my hot water bottle; it's very cold tonight."

20. **Have a natter**

Meaning: To have a chat.

Example: "Let's have a natter over coffee."

Translation: "Let's have a chat over coffee."

I

1. **Iffy**
   Meaning: Uncertain or questionable.
   Example: "That plan sounds a bit iffy to me."
   Translation: "That plan seems a bit uncertain to me."

2. **In the wop-wops**
   Meaning: In a remote or rural area.
   Example: "They live way out in the wop-wops."
   Translation: "They live far away in a remote area."

3. **It'll be right**
   Meaning: Everything will be okay or fine.
   Example: "Don't worry about it, mate, it'll be right."
   Translation: "Don't worry about it; everything will be fine."

4. **Ice block**
   Meaning: A popsicle or frozen treat on a stick.
   Example: "Let's grab an ice block from the dairy."
   Translation: "Let's get a popsicle from the corner store."

5. **Into it**
   Meaning: Enthusiastic or interested.
   Example: "He's really into it when it comes to rugby."
   Translation: "He's really enthusiastic about rugby."

6. **In the drink**
   Meaning: In the water, especially unintentionally.
   Example: "I slipped and ended up in the

drink."
Translation: "I slipped and fell into the water."

7. **In good nick**
Meaning: In good condition or shape.
Example: "That car's still in good nick for its age."
Translation: "That car is still in good condition for its age."

8. **I reckon**
Meaning: I think or believe.
Example: "I reckon we'll win the match tomorrow."
Translation: "I think we'll win the match tomorrow."

9. **In the zone**
Meaning: Focused and performing well.
Example: "She was really in the zone during her presentation."
Translation: "She was very focused and performing well during her presentation."

10. **I'm keen**
Meaning: I'm interested or eager.
Example: "There's a hike tomorrow. I'm keen!"
Translation: "There's a hike tomorrow. I'm interested!"

11. **It's a goer**
Meaning: It's likely to succeed or happen.
Example: "The new project? It's a goer!"
Translation: "The new project? It's likely to succeed!"

12. **Inside joke**
Meaning: A joke understood only by a specific group.
Example: "That's an inside joke from our road trip."

Translation: "That's a joke only our group from the road trip understands."

13. **In one ear and out the other**
Meaning: Not paying attention or retaining information.
Example: "I told him the rules, but it went in one ear and out the other."
Translation: "I explained the rules, but he didn't pay attention."

14. **I'm all ears**
Meaning: Fully listening and paying attention.
Example: "Tell me what happened; I'm all ears."
Translation: "Tell me what happened; I'm listening closely."

15. **It's all go**
Meaning: Busy or hectic.
Example: "With the new job and the move, it's all go."
Translation: "With the new job and the move, everything is hectic."

16. **In a jiffy**
Meaning: Very quickly or soon.
Example: "I'll be back in a jiffy."
Translation: "I'll return very soon."

17. **Iron out**
Meaning: To resolve or fix an issue.
Example: "We need to iron out the details before the event."
Translation: "We need to resolve the details before the event."

18. **It's mint**
Meaning: It's excellent or perfect.
Example: "This new surfboard is mint!"
Translation: "This new surfboard is excellent!"

19. **In the bag**
    Meaning: Certain or guaranteed to happen.
    Example: "With that performance, the trophy's in the bag."
    Translation: "With that performance, the trophy is guaranteed."
20. **It's a shocker**
    Meaning: Terrible or very bad.
    Example: "That game was a shocker; we played so poorly."
    Translation: "That game was terrible; we played very badly."

J

1. **Jandals**
   Meaning: Flip-flops or sandals.
   Example: "Don't forget your jandals for the beach."
   Translation: "Don't forget your flip-flops for the beach."

2. **Jack up**
   Meaning: Organize or arrange something.
   Example: "Can you jack up a ride to the concert?"
   Translation: "Can you arrange a ride to the concert?"

3. **Judder bar**
   Meaning: A speed bump.
   Example: "Slow down, there's a judder bar ahead."
   Translation: "Slow down, there's a speed bump ahead."

4. **Joker**
   Meaning: A guy, often used casually.
   Example: "That joker at the café was pretty funny."
   Translation: "That guy at the café was quite funny."

5. **Jump the queue**
   Meaning: Skip ahead in a line.
   Example: "No way you're jumping the queue, mate!"
   Translation: "You're not skipping the line, friend!"

6. **Just a tick**
   Meaning: Wait a moment or hold on.

Example: "Just a tick, I'll grab my bag."
Translation: "Wait a moment; I'll get my bag."

7. **Joker's wild**
Meaning: Unpredictable or chaotic.
Example: "The weather's joker's wild today."
Translation: "The weather is unpredictable today."

8. **Jam-packed**
Meaning: Completely full or crowded.
Example: "The concert was jam-packed last night."
Translation: "The concert was very crowded last night."

9. **Jet-lagged**
Meaning: Tired from a time zone change due to travel.
Example: "I'm so jet-lagged after that long flight."
Translation: "I'm very tired after the long flight due to the time difference."

10. **Jump in boots and all**
Meaning: Fully commit to something.
Example: "He jumped in boots and all with the new project."
Translation: "He fully committed to the new project."

11. **Jolly**
Meaning: Very or extremely (used for emphasis).
Example: "It's a jolly good day for a picnic."
Translation: "It's a very good day for a picnic."

12. **Jitters**
Meaning: Nervousness or anxiety.
Example: "She had the jitters before her speech."

Translation: "She was nervous before her speech."

13. **Jack of all trades**
Meaning: A person skilled in many areas.
Example: "He's a real jack of all trades, can fix anything."
Translation: "He's very skilled in many areas and can fix anything."

14. **Jumpy**
Meaning: Easily startled or nervous.
Example: "She's been a bit jumpy since watching that scary movie."
Translation: "She's been easily startled since watching that scary movie."

15. **Joking, mate**
Meaning: Just kidding.
Example: "Relax, I was only joking, mate."
Translation: "Relax, I was only kidding, friend."

16. **Johnny-on-the-spot**
Meaning: Someone who is always present or ready.
Example: "Thanks for helping out, Johnny-on-the-spot!"
Translation: "Thanks for being ready to help!"

17. **Jammy**
Meaning: Lucky or fortunate.
Example: "He's so jammy, winning the raffle twice!"
Translation: "He's so lucky to win the raffle twice!"

18. **Jazzed up**
Meaning: Made more exciting or lively.
Example: "We jazzed up the living room with some new cushions."

Translation: "We made the living room more lively with some new cushions."

19. **Juice**

Meaning: Electricity or energy.

Example: "The battery's out of juice; we need to charge it."

Translation: "The battery is dead; we need to charge it."

20. **Jump ship**

Meaning: Leave or abandon something, like a project or team.

Example: "He jumped ship just when things got tough."

Translation: "He abandoned the project just when it became difficult."

K

1. **Keen as**
   Meaning: Very eager or excited.
   Example: "I'm keen as to go hiking this weekend."
   Translation: "I'm very excited to go hiking this weekend."

2. **Kiwi**
   Meaning: A New Zealander, also the national bird.
   Example: "He's a proud Kiwi, born and bred."
   Translation: "He's a proud New Zealander, born and raised."

3. **Knackered**
   Meaning: Extremely tired or exhausted.
   Example: "I'm knackered after that long day at work."
   Translation: "I'm very tired after the long day at work."

4. **Kick off**
   Meaning: To start something.
   Example: "The meeting will kick off at 10 a.m."
   Translation: "The meeting will start at 10 a.m."

5. **Knock-off time**
   Meaning: The end of the workday.
   Example: "It's knock-off time; let's head to the pub."
   Translation: "It's the end of the workday; let's go to the pub."

6. **Ka pai**
   Meaning: Māori for "good" or "well done."
   Example: "Ka pai on finishing your project!"

Translation: "Well done on finishing your project!"

7. **Kick up a stink**

Meaning: To make a big fuss or complain.

Example: "She'll kick up a stink if her order's late."

Translation: "She'll complain a lot if her order is late."

8. **Koru**

Meaning: A Māori spiral design symbolizing new beginnings.

Example: "The koru design on that carving is beautiful."

Translation: "The spiral design on that carving is beautiful."

9. **Kiwifruit**

Meaning: A fruit with green flesh and a furry brown skin.

Example: "We'll have kiwifruit for dessert."

Translation: "We'll eat kiwifruit for dessert."

10. **Kickback**

Meaning: To relax or unwind.

Example: "Let's kickback and enjoy the sunshine."

Translation: "Let's relax and enjoy the sunshine."

11. **Kina**

Meaning: A type of sea urchin, often eaten as a delicacy.

Example: "We gathered kina on the beach this morning."

Translation: "We collected sea urchins on the beach this morning."

12. **Knock your socks off**

Meaning: To amaze or impress someone.

Example: "This dessert will knock your socks off."
Translation: "This dessert will impress you greatly."

13. **Kick it to touch**
Meaning: Postpone or avoid dealing with something.
Example: "We'll kick it to touch and revisit later."
Translation: "We'll postpone it and revisit it later."

14. **Knock back**
Meaning: To refuse or reject something.
Example: "They knocked back my idea for the project."
Translation: "They rejected my idea for the project."

15. **Kiwiana**
Meaning: Items or cultural elements iconic to New Zealand.
Example: "Jandals and pavlova are classic Kiwiana."
Translation: "Flip-flops and pavlova are iconic New Zealand elements."

16. **Knock up**
Meaning: To quickly prepare something.
Example: "I'll knock up a salad for dinner."
Translation: "I'll quickly make a salad for dinner."

17. **Kicked the bucket**
Meaning: Passed away or died.
Example: "The old fridge finally kicked the bucket."
Translation: "The old fridge finally stopped working."

18. **Keep your cool**

Meaning: Stay calm and composed.
Example: "Even under pressure, he kept his cool."
Translation: "Even under pressure, he stayed calm."

19. **Kōrero**

Meaning: Māori for "conversation" or "discussion."
Example: "Let's have a kōrero about the plan."
Translation: "Let's have a discussion about the plan."

20. **Kick the habit**

Meaning: To stop doing something, often a bad habit.
Example: "He's trying to kick the habit of smoking."
Translation: "He's trying to stop smoking."

L

1. **L&P (Lemon & Paeroa)**
   Meaning: A popular fizzy drink in New Zealand.
   Example: "Grab a bottle of L&P for the barbecue."
   Translation: "Get a bottle of Lemon & Paeroa for the barbecue."

2. **Larrikin**
   Meaning: A mischievous or playful person.
   Example: "He's such a larrikin, always making us laugh."
   Translation: "He's so mischievous, always making us laugh."

3. **Long drop**
   Meaning: A basic outdoor toilet.
   Example: "The bach has a long drop out the back."
   Translation: "The holiday home has an outdoor toilet behind it."

4. **Low-key**
   Meaning: Simple, understated, or quiet.
   Example: "We're having a low-key get-together tonight."
   Translation: "We're having a simple gathering tonight."

5. **Lush**
   Meaning: Beautiful or appealing, often used for nature.
   Example: "The forest here is so lush after the rain."
   Translation: "The forest here is very beautiful after the rain."

6. **Lock-up**
   Meaning: A small storage space or shed.
   Example: "All the tools are in the lock-up."
   Translation: "All the tools are in the storage shed."
7. **Loaf around**
   Meaning: To be lazy or idle.
   Example: "He's just loafing around on the couch all day."
   Translation: "He's just being lazy on the couch all day."
8. **Lippy**
   Meaning: Talking back or being cheeky.
   Example: "Don't get lippy with your parents."
   Translation: "Don't talk back to your parents."
9. **Lost the plot**
   Meaning: Acting irrationally or unusually.
   Example: "He's completely lost the plot over that argument."
   Translation: "He's behaving irrationally because of that argument."
10. **Laid-back**
    Meaning: Relaxed and easy-going.
    Example: "Kiwis are known for their laid-back lifestyle."
    Translation: "New Zealanders are known for their relaxed way of life."
11. **Loaded**
    Meaning: Wealthy or rich.
    Example: "He's loaded, drives a new car every year."
    Translation: "He's rich and buys a new car every year."
12. **Lucky dip**
    Meaning: A random choice or selection.

Example: "The prizes at the fair were a lucky dip."
Translation: "The prizes at the fair were chosen randomly."

13. **Log off**
Meaning: Disconnect from the internet or take a break.
Example: "You should log off and get some fresh air."
Translation: "You should disconnect and spend time outside."

14. **Leg it**
Meaning: To run away quickly.
Example: "When the dog barked, he legged it out of there."
Translation: "When the dog barked, he ran away quickly."

15. **Left field**
Meaning: Unexpected or unconventional.
Example: "That suggestion came out of left field."
Translation: "That suggestion was unexpected."

16. **Light as a feather**
Meaning: Very lightweight.
Example: "This new phone is light as a feather."
Translation: "This new phone is extremely lightweight."

17. **Lad**
Meaning: A young man or boy.
Example: "That lad's got some serious rugby skills."
Translation: "That boy has impressive rugby skills."

18. **Loopy**
Meaning: Crazy or eccentric.
Example: "The idea sounds a bit loopy, but it might work."
Translation: "The idea seems a bit crazy, but it might work."

19. **Legless**
Meaning: Extremely drunk.
Example: "He got legless at the party last night."
Translation: "He got very drunk at the party last night."

20. **Looker**
Meaning: An attractive person.
Example: "She's a real looker, isn't she?"
Translation: "She's very attractive, don't you think?"

M

1. **Mate**
   Meaning: Friend or buddy, often used casually
   Example: "Thanks for helping me out, mate."
   Translation: "Thanks for helping me out, friend."

2. **Munted**
   Meaning: Broken, ruined, or intoxicated.
   Example: "The car's munted after that crash."
   Translation: "The car is ruined after that crash."

3. **Mooch around**
   Meaning: Wander aimlessly or loaf about.
   Example: "I'm just going to mooch around town today."
   Translation: "I'm just going to wander around town today."

4. **Mana**
   Meaning: Māori word for prestige, authority, or respect.
   Example: "He's got a lot of mana in the community."
   Translation: "He has a lot of respect in the community."

5. **Mozzie**
   Meaning: Mosquito.
   Example: "The mozzies are bad tonight, grab the repellent."
   Translation: "The mosquitoes are bad tonight, get the repellent."

6. **Munty**
   Meaning: Ugly or unpleasant.

Example: "That's a pretty munty old chair."
Translation: "That's a rather ugly old chair."

7. **Mission**
   Meaning: A long or difficult task.
   Example: "It was a mission to get up that hill."
   Translation: "It was a difficult task to climb that hill."

8. **Ministry of Works**
   Meaning: A slow or inefficient process, often jokingly.
   Example: "It's like the Ministry of Works trying to fix that road."
   Translation: "It's as slow as a bureaucratic process fixing that road."

9. **Main drag**
   Meaning: The main street of a town or city.
   Example: "We'll meet on the main drag at 7."
   Translation: "We'll meet on the main street at 7."

10. **Mahi**
    Meaning: Māori word for work.
    Example: "I've got heaps of mahi to finish today."
    Translation: "I have a lot of work to finish today."

11. **Manky**
    Meaning: Dirty or unpleasant.
    Example: "This shirt's too manky to wear again."
    Translation: "This shirt is too dirty to wear again."

12. **Milk bar**
    Meaning: A small shop selling snacks and drinks.
    Example: "Let's grab an ice cream from the

milk bar."
Translation: "Let's get an ice cream from the snack shop."

13. **Moolah**
Meaning: Money.
Example: "I need to save some moolah for the trip."
Translation: "I need to save some money for the trip."

14. **Mean as**
Meaning: Awesome or excellent.
Example: "That concert was mean as last night!"
Translation: "That concert was awesome last night!"

15. **Munted out**
Meaning: Exhausted or worn out.
Example: "I'm completely munted out after the hike."
Translation: "I'm completely exhausted after the hike."

16. **Mate's rates**
Meaning: A discount or favor given to friends.
Example: "I got my car fixed for mate's rates."
Translation: "I got my car fixed at a discount because of friendship."

17. **Meat pie**
Meaning: A classic Kiwi snack, often with beef filling.
Example: "I'll grab a meat pie for lunch."
Translation: "I'll get a meat pie for lunch."

18. **Massive**
Meaning: Big or great in importance.
Example: "That game was massive for the team."

Translation: "That game was very important for the team."

19. **Mash up**

Meaning: Mix together, often in music or ideas.

Example: "The DJ did a cool mash-up of old and new hits."

Translation: "The DJ mixed old and new hits creatively."

20. **Mickey Mouse**

Meaning: Excellent or first-rate.

Example: "That new car is Mickey Mouse, mate!"

Translation: "That new car is excellent, friend!"

N

1. **Nana**
Meaning: Grandmother or elderly woman.
Example: "We're visiting Nana this weekend."
Translation: "We're visiting Grandma this weekend."

2. **Nark**
Meaning: Someone who tattles or complains.
Example: "Don't be such a nark about the noise."
Translation: "Don't complain so much about the noise."

3. **Nek minute**
Meaning: "Next minute," used to describe a sudden or unexpected change.
Example: "I was relaxing on the beach, nek minute it started raining."
Translation: "I was relaxing on the beach, then suddenly it started raining."

4. **Nifty**
Meaning: Handy, clever, or stylish.
Example: "That's a nifty little gadget you've got there."
Translation: "That's a clever little gadget you have there."

5. **No worries**
Meaning: It's fine; no problem.
Example: "Thanks for helping! No worries, mate."
Translation: "Thanks for helping! It's no problem, friend."

6. **Naff**
Meaning: Lame, uncool, or unimpressive.

Example: "That movie was a bit naff."
Translation: "That movie was a bit unimpressive."

7. **No drama**
Meaning: No problem; everything's okay.
Example: "I'll fix it for you. No drama."
Translation: "I'll fix it for you. It's no problem."

8. **Nutter**
Meaning: A crazy or eccentric person.
Example: "That guy running in the rain is a bit of a nutter."
Translation: "That guy running in the rain is a bit crazy."

9. **Nudge**
Meaning: A slight push or encouragement.
Example: "Give me a nudge if I fall asleep during the movie."
Translation: "Give me a light push if I fall asleep during the movie."

10. **Not even**
Meaning: Expression of disbelief or rejection.
Example: "Did you finish the project? Not even!"
Translation: "Did you finish the project? Definitely not!"

11. **Na mate**
Meaning: Goodbye, often in a casual or friendly tone.
Example: "See you tomorrow. Na mate!"
Translation: "See you tomorrow. Bye, friend!"

12. **No sweat**
Meaning: Easy or not a problem.
Example: "Thanks for carrying the groceries. No sweat!"

Translation: "Thanks for carrying the groceries. It was no problem!"

13. **Noodle around**
Meaning: To play or experiment, often with ideas or objects.
Example: "He's been noodling around with that guitar all day."
Translation: "He's been experimenting with that guitar all day."

14. **Nailed it**
Meaning: Successfully accomplished something.
Example: "You nailed it with that speech!"
Translation: "You did an excellent job with that speech!"

15. **Naff off**
Meaning: Go away or leave, used rudely or jokingly.
Example: "Naff off, I'm trying to concentrate."
Translation: "Go away, I'm trying to concentrate."

16. **Not my cup of tea**
Meaning: Not something I enjoy or prefer.
Example: "Horror movies aren't my cup of tea."
Translation: "I don't enjoy horror movies."

17. **Nice one**
Meaning: Well done or good job.
Example: "You found my keys! Nice one!"
Translation: "You found my keys! Good job!"

18. **Nope**
Meaning: Informal way of saying no.
Example: "Are you going to the party? Nope."
Translation: "Are you going to the party? No."

19. **Naffy**
    Meaning: Silly or foolish.
    Example: "That's such a naffy excuse."
    Translation: "That's such a foolish excuse."
20. **Number eight wire**
    Meaning: A symbol of Kiwi ingenuity and improvisation.
    Example: "We fixed the fence with a bit of number eight wire."
    Translation: "We fixed the fence with a creative solution."

O

1. **Oosh**
   Meaning: Expression of excitement or surprise.
   Example: "Oosh, that was an awesome goal!"
   Translation: "Wow, that was an amazing goal!"

2. **Oi**
   Meaning: Hey, or used to get someone's attention.
   Example: "Oi, pass me the remote!"
   Translation: "Hey, pass me the remote!"

3. **On the piss**
   Meaning: Drinking alcohol, usually heavily.
   Example: "We were on the piss all weekend."
   Translation: "We were drinking a lot all weekend."

4. **Off chop**
   Meaning: To leave quickly or abruptly.
   Example: "I'm off chop, catch you later!"
   Translation: "I'm leaving quickly, see you later!"

5. **Out of it**
   Meaning: Drunk, high, or extremely tired.
   Example: "She was totally out of it after the party."
   Translation: "She was completely out of it after the party."

6. **Owl**
   Meaning: Someone who stays up late at night.
   Example: "He's such an owl, always up at 2 AM."
   Translation: "He stays up so late, always awake at 2 AM."

7. **On the mend**
   Meaning: Recovering from an illness or injury.
   Example: "He's on the mend after the surgery."
   Translation: "He's recovering after the surgery."

8. **Over the moon**
   Meaning: Extremely happy or excited.
   Example: "She was over the moon when she got the job."
   Translation: "She was extremely happy when she got the job."

9. **Off the rails**
   Meaning: Acting in a disorganized or reckless way.
   Example: "He's been off the rails since the breakup."
   Translation: "He's been acting recklessly since the breakup."

10. **Oath**
    Meaning: A strong affirmation or agreement.
    Example: "I swear on my oath, I'll finish it tomorrow."
    Translation: "I swear, I'll finish it tomorrow."

11. **Ouch**
    Meaning: Expression of pain or surprise.
    Example: "Ouch, that hurt!"
    Translation: "That really hurt!"

12. **Old school**
    Meaning: Traditional or classic, often with a sense of respect.
    Example: "That old school music is my favorite."
    Translation: "That traditional music is my favorite."

13. **Off the cuff**
Meaning: Spontaneous, without preparation.
Example: "He gave an off-the-cuff speech at the wedding."
Translation: "He gave a spontaneous speech at the wedding."

14. **On a roll**
Meaning: Having a series of successes or good luck.
Example: "She's on a roll with her projects at work."
Translation: "She's having great success with her projects at work."

15. **Out of pocket**
Meaning: To be financially inconvenienced, or unable to attend.
Example: "I'm a bit out of pocket after the trip."
Translation: "I'm financially stretched after the trip."

16. **On the go**
Meaning: Busy or active.
Example: "She's always on the go, never stops."
Translation: "She's always busy, never stops."

17. **Over it**
Meaning: Tired of or no longer interested in something.
Example: "I'm so over this rainy weather!"
Translation: "I'm tired of this rainy weather!"

18. **Out of sight**
Meaning: Something really impressive or amazing.
Example: "That sunset was out of sight!"
Translation: "That sunset was incredible!"

19. **Out of line**
    Meaning: Behaving inappropriately or disrespectfully.
    Example: "That comment was totally out of line."
    Translation: "That comment was completely inappropriate."
20. **On point**
    Meaning: Exactly right or perfectly done.
    Example: "Your presentation was on point."
    Translation: "Your presentation was perfect."

P

1. **Pine**
   Meaning: To long for or miss something.
   Example: "She's been pining for her old job."
   Translation: "She's been missing her old job."

2. **Pissed**
   Meaning: Drunk or intoxicated.
   Example: "He was so pissed after the party."
   Translation: "He was so drunk after the party."

3. **Pash**
   Meaning: A passionate kiss.
   Example: "They shared a pash at the party."
   Translation: "They shared a passionate kiss at the party."

4. **Poo**
   Meaning: Stool or feces, often used humorously.
   Example: "The dog left a poo on the lawn."
   Translation: "The dog left stool on the lawn."

5. **Pukeko**
   Meaning: A native New Zealand bird, often used to describe a clumsy person.
   Example: "He tripped over his own feet, like a pukeko!"
   Translation: "He tripped over his own feet, like a clumsy person!"

6. **Pissed off**
   Meaning: Angry or upset.
   Example: "She was really pissed off when she found out."
   Translation: "She was really angry when she found out."

7. **Penny**
   Meaning: A small amount of money, or sometimes used to describe cheapness.
   Example: "That's a penny saved for every dollar earned."
   Translation: "That's a small amount saved for every dollar earned."

8. **Pike**
   Meaning: To abandon or leave something unexpectedly.
   Example: "He pike-ed out before we could leave."
   Translation: "He left without warning before we could leave."

9. **Piss take**
   Meaning: To make fun of or tease someone.
   Example: "Stop the piss take, I'm serious!"
   Translation: "Stop teasing, I'm serious!"

10. **Pick up**
    Meaning: To improve or get better.
    Example: "Things will pick up once we finish this project."
    Translation: "Things will improve once we finish this project."

11. **Pigeon**
    Meaning: A naive or gullible person.
    Example: "He's such a pigeon for falling for that scam."
    Translation: "He's so gullible for falling for that scam."

12. **Pavlova**
    Meaning: A famous Kiwi dessert made of meringue and fruit.
    Example: "She made the best pavlova for Christmas."

Translation: "She made the best meringue dessert for Christmas."

13. **Puckered up**
Meaning: To make a kissing face.
Example: "She puckered up when he leaned in."
Translation: "She made a kissing face when he leaned in."

14. **Pooing in the woods**
Meaning: Doing something that seems odd or out of place, often referring to an outdoor activity.
Example: "I had to go pooing in the woods after the hike."
Translation: "I had to do something odd, like pooping in the woods after the hike."

15. **Paddy**
Meaning: A fit of anger or temper tantrum.
Example: "Don't have a paddy just because things aren't going your way."
Translation: "Don't throw a temper tantrum just because things aren't going your way."

16. **Porkies**
Meaning: Lies or fibs.
Example: "Stop telling porkies, we know the truth."
Translation: "Stop telling lies, we know the truth."

17. **Punter**
Meaning: A customer, often used for people who gamble or attend events.
Example: "The punters are all lining up for tickets."
Translation: "The customers are all lining up for tickets."

18. **Pash rash**
    Meaning: The redness or irritation on the face after an intense kiss.
    Example: "He had pash rash after their date."
    Translation: "He had redness on his face after their date."
19. **Poo face**
    Meaning: A sulky or upset expression.
    Example: "Why are you pulling a poo face?"
    Translation: "Why are you looking upset?"
20. **Put the boot in**
    Meaning: To criticize or make things worse, especially when someone is already down.
    Example: "Stop putting the boot in; he's already had a tough day."
    Translation: "Stop criticizing; he's already had a tough day."

Q

1. **Quid**
   Meaning: A term for money, typically referring to pounds in the UK, but can be used in NZ for cash.
   Example: "I need a few quid to grab a drink."
   Translation: "I need a few dollars to grab a drink."

2. **Quake**
   Meaning: An earthquake, often used in reference to New Zealand's seismic activity.
   Example: "We had a big quake last night."
   Translation: "We had a big earthquake last night."

3. **Quirky**
   Meaning: Unconventional or unusual in a charming way.
   Example: "She's got a quirky sense of humor."
   Translation: "She has an unconventional sense of humor."

4. **Quick as a flash**
   Meaning: Very fast or speedy.
   Example: "I'll be there quick as a flash!"
   Translation: "I'll be there really quickly!"

5. **Queer**
   Meaning: A term that can refer to something strange or unusual, but also used as a respectful term for LGBTQ+ individuals.
   Example: "That's a bit queer, isn't it?"
   Translation: "That's a bit strange, isn't it?"

6. **Quash**
   Meaning: To cancel, suppress, or reject something.

Example: "The decision was quashed by the court."
Translation: "The decision was canceled by the court."

7. **Queue up**
   Meaning: To wait in line or to line up.
   Example: "We had to queue up for ages at the concert."
   Translation: "We had to wait in line for a long time at the concert."

8. **Quid's in**
   Meaning: A phrase indicating that someone is in a good financial situation, or has money coming their way.
   Example: "If that deal goes through, the quid's in!"
   Translation: "If that deal goes through, they will be in a good financial position!"

9. **Quick off the mark**
   Meaning: Someone who is fast to react or take action.
   Example: "You were quick off the mark with that response!"
   Translation: "You were fast to respond!"

10. **Quite the opposite**
    Meaning: A phrase used when something is completely different or contrary to what was expected.
    Example: "You think it's expensive, but it's quite the opposite!"
    Translation: "You think it's expensive, but it's actually quite cheap!"

11. **Quaint**
    Meaning: Charming, old-fashioned, or unusual in a pleasing way.

Example: "That little cottage is so quaint."
Translation: "That little cottage is so charming."

12. **Quick fix**
Meaning: A temporary or easy solution to a problem.
Example: "That's just a quick fix; it won't solve the issue long term."
Translation: "That's just a temporary solution; it won't solve the problem for long."

13. **Quarrel**
Meaning: An argument or dispute.
Example: "They had a big quarrel over the project."
Translation: "They had a big argument over the project."

14. **Quality time**
Meaning: Time spent meaningfully with someone.
Example: "We need some quality time together this weekend."
Translation: "We need to spend meaningful time together this weekend."

15. **Quantify**
Meaning: To measure or express something in numerical terms.
Example: "It's hard to quantify how much effort I've put into this."
Translation: "It's hard to measure how much effort I've put into this."

16. **Quench**
Meaning: To satisfy thirst or put out a fire.
Example: "A cold drink will quench your thirst."

Translation: "A cold drink will satisfy your thirst."

17. **Quick-witted**
Meaning: Someone who can think and respond quickly, often with humor.
Example: "She's really quick-witted in conversations."
Translation: "She's very clever in conversations."

18. **Quibble**
Meaning: To argue or complain about something trivial.
Example: "Stop quibbling about the details, let's get on with it!"
Translation: "Stop arguing about the details, let's continue!"

19. **Quaint as**
Meaning: Very charming or old-fashioned, typically used for things that are nostalgic or cute.
Example: "The town is quaint as."
Translation: "The town is very charming."

20. **Quarantine**
Meaning: To isolate someone or something due to potential infection, often used in reference to health or safety.
Example: "The animals had to be put into quarantine when they arrived."
Translation: "The animals had to be isolated when they arrived."

R

1. **Rattle your dags**
   Meaning: Hurry up or move quickly.
   Example: "Rattle your dags, we're going to be late!"
   Translation: "Hurry up, we're going to be late!'

2. **Rooted**
   Meaning: Extremely tired or worn out, or also used to refer to something broken or ruined.
   Example: "I'm absolutely rooted after that workout."
   Translation: "I'm completely exhausted after that workout."

3. **Ragged**
   Meaning: Something that is in bad condition or torn, also can refer to being worn out.
   Example: "Those shoes are looking pretty ragged."
   Translation: "Those shoes are looking worn out."

4. **Reckon**
   Meaning: To think or believe something.
   Example: "I reckon we'll get there by 5 PM."
   Translation: "I think we'll get there by 5 PM."

5. **Reo**
   Meaning: Short for "te reo Māori," which refers to the Māori language.
   Example: "He speaks some reo Māori."
   Translation: "He speaks some Māori language."

6. **Rookie**
   Meaning: A beginner or someone new to a job or activity.

Example: "She's a rookie at this job but learning fast."
Translation: "She's new to this job but learning quickly."

7. **Rattle**
Meaning: To make a noise, or to be shaken or unsettled.
Example: "The noise from the truck really rattled me."
Translation: "The noise from the truck really scared me."

8. **Rubbish**
Meaning: Trash or something of poor quality.
Example: "This movie is just rubbish!"
Translation: "This movie is terrible!"

9. **Rug up**
Meaning: To dress warmly, especially in cold weather.
Example: "Make sure you rug up before going outside."
Translation: "Make sure you dress warmly before going outside."

10. **Rough as guts**
Meaning: Something or someone that is very rough or unrefined.
Example: "That pub is rough as guts, you wouldn't want to go there."
Translation: "That pub is very unrefined, you wouldn't want to go there."

11. **Reckon on**
Meaning: To count on or rely on something happening.
Example: "I wouldn't reckon on them arriving on time."

Translation: "I wouldn't rely on them arriving on time."

12. **Rough it**

Meaning: To live or travel in a way that is uncomfortable or basic.

Example: "We had to rough it on the camping trip with no showers."

Translation: "We had to live in basic conditions on the camping trip with no showers."

13. **Roll your sleeves up**

Meaning: To prepare for hard work or to get involved in a challenging task.

Example: "Time to roll your sleeves up and get to work!"

Translation: "Time to prepare for hard work and get started!"

14. **Ring around**

Meaning: To make phone calls to multiple people, usually to get information or gather a group.

Example: "I'll ring around to see who's available for the meeting."

Translation: "I'll call around to see who's available for the meeting."

15. **Riding shotgun**

Meaning: Sitting in the front passenger seat of a vehicle.

Example: "I'm riding shotgun, so I get to choose the music!"

Translation: "I'm sitting in the front seat, so I get to choose the music!"

16. **Rant**

Meaning: To speak or shout at length in a passionate or angry way.

Example: "He went on a rant about the new policy."

Translation: "He went on a long, angry speech about the new policy."

17. **Rook it**

Meaning: To cheat, deceive, or trick someone.

Example: "Don't try to rook me out of my share of the winnings!"

Translation: "Don't try to cheat me out of my share of the winnings!"

18. **Rage quit**

Meaning: To quit something, usually a game or task, in anger or frustration.

Example: "He rage quit the game when he lost."

Translation: "He quit the game in anger when he lost."

19. **Right as rain**

Meaning: To feel fine, healthy, or okay.

Example: "Don't worry, I'm right as rain after that cold."

Translation: "I'm perfectly fine after that cold."

20. **Redneck**

Meaning: Referring to someone from a rural background, often used to describe someone perceived as unsophisticated or country-like.

Example: "He's a bit of a redneck with his love of hunting and trucks."

Translation: "He's a bit of a country person with his love of hunting and trucks."

S

1. **Sweet as**
   Meaning: Something that is really great, cool, or perfect.
   Example: "That new song is sweet as!"
   Translation: "That new song is really great!"
2. **Shark**
   Meaning: A skilled or talented person, often used for someone who is very good at a particular activity.
   Example: "He's a shark at poker."
   Translation: "He's really good at poker."
3. **Suss**
   Meaning: To figure something out or to investigate.
   Example: "I've sussed out the problem with the car."
   Translation: "I've figured out the problem with the car."
4. **Skux**
   Meaning: A term for someone who is cool or attractive, often used in reference to someone who is smooth or charming.
   Example: "He's such a skux, all the girls love him."
   Translation: "He's so attractive, everyone loves him."
5. **Stoked**
   Meaning: Excited or thrilled about something.
   Example: "I'm stoked for the concert tonight!"
   Translation: "I'm excited for the concert tonight!"
6. **Skint**
   Meaning: Broke or having no money.

Example: "I can't go out tonight, I'm skint."
Translation: "I can't go out tonight, I'm broke."

7. **Snog**
   Meaning: To kiss, often used in reference to passionate kissing.
   Example: "They were snogging all night at the party."
   Translation: "They were kissing passionately all night at the party."

8. **Stingy**
   Meaning: Unwilling to spend money or share.
   Example: "Don't be stingy, buy a round of drinks!"
   Translation: "Don't be cheap, buy a round of drinks!"

9. **Sorted**
   Meaning: Organized or taken care of, often used when everything is in place.
   Example: "Don't worry, I've got it all sorted."
   Translation: "Don't worry, I've organized everything."

10. **Sick**
    Meaning: Something that is very cool or impressive.
    Example: "That skateboard trick was sick!"
    Translation: "That skateboard trick was amazing!"

11. **Shonky**
    Meaning: Something that is of poor quality or dishonest.
    Example: "The mechanic gave me a shonky deal."
    Translation: "The mechanic gave me a poor deal."

12. **Suss out**
    Meaning: To figure out or understand something.
    Example: "I'll suss out what's going on and let you know."
    Translation: "I'll figure out what's going on and let you know."

13. **Sickie**
    Meaning: A day off from work or school when one is pretending to be sick.
    Example: "He's taking a sickie to go to the beach."
    Translation: "He's taking a day off to go to the beach."

14. **Smoko**
    Meaning: A break or rest, especially during work hours.
    Example: "It's smoko time, let's take a break."
    Translation: "It's break time, let's take a rest."

15. **Shag**
    Meaning: To have sexual intercourse, often used casually.
    Example: "They had a shag after the party."
    Translation: "They had sex after the party."

16. **Stoked up**
    Meaning: To be prepared or excited about something.
    Example: "We're all stoked up for the big game."
    Translation: "We're all excited for the big game."

17. **Slack**
    Meaning: Lazy or not putting in enough effort.
    Example: "Stop being slack and finish your work!"

Translation: "Stop being lazy and finish your work!"

18. **Squiz**

Meaning: To take a quick look at something.
Example: "Give us a squiz at that report."
Translation: "Give us a quick look at that report."

19. **Snap**

Meaning: To take a photograph.
Example: "Can you snap a picture of us?"
Translation: "Can you take a photograph of us?"

20. **Shut the gate**

Meaning: Used to express surprise, often in a humorous way.
Example: "Shut the gate, I can't believe they're getting married!"
Translation: "I can't believe they're getting married!"

T

1. **Tiki tour**
   Meaning: A detour or a long, scenic route, often taken for enjoyment rather than efficiency.
   Example: "We took a tiki tour through the countryside to see the sights."
   Translation: "We took a scenic detour through the countryside to see the sights."

2. **Tiki**
   Meaning: A term used for a carved wooden figure representing Māori culture, or a style associated with it.
   Example: "We bought a small tiki from the market as a souvenir."
   Translation: "We bought a small carved figure from the market as a souvenir."

3. **Tucker**
   Meaning: Food, often used in a casual or colloquial sense.
   Example: "Let's grab some tucker before the game."
   Translation: "Let's grab some food before the game."

4. **Twee**
   Meaning: Something overly cute, quaint, or cloying.
   Example: "That's a bit twee for my taste."
   Translation: "That's a bit too cute or precious for my taste."

5. **Tight**
   Meaning: Used to describe someone who is frugal or unwilling to spend money.
   Example: "He's too tight to buy a round of

drinks."
Translation: "He's too stingy to buy a round of drinks."

6. **Ta**
Meaning: A casual way to say "thank you."
Example: "Ta for helping me out today!"
Translation: "Thanks for helping me out today!"

7. **Tomo**
Meaning: A friend or mate, often used affectionately.
Example: "I'm going out with my tomo this weekend."
Translation: "I'm going out with my friend this weekend."

8. **Throw a wobbly**
Meaning: To lose one's temper or have a tantrum.
Example: "She threw a wobbly when she didn't get her way."
Translation: "She had a tantrum when she didn't get her way."

9. **Tough as old boots**
Meaning: Very strong or durable, often used to describe a person or thing that is tough and unyielding.
Example: "He's tough as old boots, nothing can stop him."
Translation: "He's very tough, nothing can stop him."

10. **Take the mickey**
Meaning: To tease or mock someone, often in a playful way.
Example: "Stop taking the mickey out of her,

she's sensitive."

Translation: "Stop teasing her, she's sensitive."

11. **Tidy**

Meaning: Used to describe something that is neat, nice, or impressive.

Example: "That's a tidy little car you've got there."

Translation: "That's a nice little car you've got there."

12. **Tussle**

Meaning: A minor, physical struggle or fight.

Example: "The kids had a tussle over the last piece of cake."

Translation: "The kids had a minor struggle over the last piece of cake."

13. **Tight-arse**

Meaning: A very stingy person who avoids spending money.

Example: "Don't ask John for a loan, he's a tight-arse."

Translation: "Don't ask John for a loan, he's very stingy."

14. **Tack**

Meaning: To change course or approach, often used in terms of strategy.

Example: "I had to tack to a new plan when the first one failed."

Translation: "I had to change my approach when the first one failed."

15. **Take the piss**

Meaning: To make fun of someone or something in a mocking way.

Example: "You're just taking the piss now!"

Translation: "You're just mocking me now!"

16. **Teed off**
    Meaning: To be annoyed or angry about something.
    Example: "He's really teed off about losing his job."
    Translation: "He's really angry about losing his job."

17. **Tramping**
    Meaning: Hiking or backpacking, often used in the context of New Zealand's outdoor activities.
    Example: "We're going tramping in the mountains this weekend."
    Translation: "We're going hiking in the mountains this weekend."

18. **Tack on**
    Meaning: To add something extra, often as an afterthought.
    Example: "I'll tack on a few extra hours to finish the work."
    Translation: "I'll add a few extra hours to finish the work."

19. **Tighten up**
    Meaning: To become stricter or more controlled.
    Example: "The rules will tighten up after the incident."
    Translation: "The rules will become stricter after the incident."

20. **Throw a spanner in the works**
    Meaning: To cause problems or disrupt plans.
    Example: "The rain threw a spanner in the works for the outdoor event."
    Translation: "The rain caused problems for the outdoor event."

U

1. **Uptight**
   Meaning: Anxious or tense, often used to describe someone who is overly nervous or rigid.
   Example: "She's a bit uptight about the presentation tomorrow."
   Translation: "She's a bit anxious about the presentation tomorrow."

2. **Usual**
   Meaning: Referring to something that is typical or standard.
   Example: "Just the usual, thanks."
   Translation: "Just the normal thing, thanks."

3. **Under the weather**
   Meaning: Feeling sick or unwell.
   Example: "I'm feeling a bit under the weather today."
   Translation: "I'm feeling a bit sick today."

4. **Up for it**
   Meaning: Willing to participate in or do something.
   Example: "Are you up for going to the beach tomorrow?"
   Translation: "Are you willing to go to the beach tomorrow?"

5. **Uphill battle**
   Meaning: A difficult or challenging task.
   Example: "Getting this project finished on time is going to be an uphill battle."
   Translation: "Getting this project finished on time is going to be very difficult."

6. **Under the radar**
   Meaning: To do something quietly or without

attracting attention.
Example: "I'm trying to keep things under the radar until I get approval."
Translation: "I'm trying to keep things low-key until I get approval."

7. **Up the creek**
Meaning: In a difficult or problematic situation.
Example: "We're up the creek without a paddle if the car breaks down here."
Translation: "We're in a tough situation if the car breaks down here."

8. **Uptick**
Meaning: A small increase, especially in a trend or situation.
Example: "There's been an uptick in sales since the promotion."
Translation: "There's been a small increase in sales since the promotion."

9. **Under your belt**
Meaning: To have gained experience or completed something successfully.
Example: "With years of experience under his belt, he's the perfect candidate for the job."
Translation: "With years of experience behind him, he's the perfect candidate for the job."

10. **Up in arms**
Meaning: To be very angry or upset about something.
Example: "The community is up in arms about the new policy."
Translation: "The community is really angry about the new policy."

11. **Up and about**
Meaning: To be active and moving around,

especially after being unwell.
Example: "She's finally up and about after being sick for a week."
Translation: "She's finally feeling better and moving around after being sick for a week."

12. **Up to scratch**
Meaning: To meet expectations or standards.
Example: "Your work isn't quite up to scratch yet."
Translation: "Your work isn't quite meeting the expected standards yet."

13. **Under lock and key**
Meaning: Something that is locked away securely or carefully guarded.
Example: "Make sure the valuables are under lock and key when you leave the house."
Translation: "Make sure the valuables are securely locked away when you leave the house."

14. **Up the ante**
Meaning: To increase the stakes or level of difficulty.
Example: "We need to up the ante in this competition if we want to win."
Translation: "We need to raise the stakes in this competition if we want to win."

15. **Unreal**
Meaning: Used to describe something that is amazing or unbelievable.
Example: "The view from the top of the mountain is unreal!"
Translation: "The view from the top of the mountain is amazing!"

16. **Uncharted territory**
Meaning: A situation that is new or unfamiliar.

Example: "This is uncharted territory for us; we've never done this before."
Translation: "This is a completely new and unfamiliar situation for us."

17. **Uptake**
Meaning: The act of understanding or absorbing information.
Example: "He's got a quick uptake, so he'll catch on to the training easily."
Translation: "He understands quickly, so he'll catch on to the training easily."

18. **Underhanded**
Meaning: Dishonest or sneaky behavior.
Example: "His underhanded tactics didn't fool anyone."
Translation: "His dishonest tactics didn't fool anyone."

19. **Until the cows come home**
Meaning: For a very long time, often used when something seems endless.
Example: "You can argue about this until the cows come home, but I won't change my mind."
Translation: "You can argue about this for a very long time, but I won't change my mind."

20. **Up to no good**
Meaning: Engaging in behavior that is dishonest or mischievous.
Example: "Those kids are up to no good, I can tell."
Translation: "Those kids are doing something mischievous, I can tell."

V

1. **Vibe**
   Meaning: The feeling or atmosphere of a place, situation, or person.
   Example: "This party has such a chill vibe."
   Translation: "This party has such a relaxed atmosphere."

2. **Vino**
   Meaning: Wine.
   Example: "Let's grab some vino for dinner."
   Translation: "Let's grab some wine for dinner."

3. **Vexed**
   Meaning: Annoyed or frustrated.
   Example: "She was really vexed when she found out the meeting was canceled."
   Translation: "She was really annoyed when she found out the meeting was canceled."

4. **Vibe killer**
   Meaning: A person or thing that ruins the good atmosphere or mood.
   Example: "Don't be such a vibe killer, let's have fun!"
   Translation: "Don't ruin the mood, let's have fun!"

5. **Vino verde**
   Meaning: A type of light, young wine, often from Portugal, used informally to refer to any wine.
   Example: "We should try some vino verde at the restaurant."
   Translation: "We should try some light wine at the restaurant."

6. **Vamoose**
   Meaning: To leave or depart quickly.

Example: "It's getting late, we better vamoose."
Translation: "It's getting late, we better leave."

7. **Vege**
Meaning: Short for vegetarian.
Example: "I'm a vege, so I'll have the tofu salad."
Translation: "I'm a vegetarian, so I'll have the tofu salad."

8. **Vulture**
Meaning: A person who takes advantage of others' misfortune, often for profit.
Example: "He's a vulture, always looking to make money off others' struggles."
Translation: "He's someone who takes advantage of others' misfortunes."

9. **Vibing**
Meaning: To be in a good mood or to enjoy something.
Example: "I'm just vibing, enjoying the music."
Translation: "I'm just enjoying the music and in a good mood."

10. **Viral**
Meaning: Something that spreads quickly or becomes widely known, usually in reference to media or online content.
Example: "That video went viral overnight!"
Translation: "That video became extremely popular overnight!"

11. **Verbal diarrhoea**
Meaning: Talking excessively without much substance, often in a rambling manner.
Example: "He has verbal diarrhoea, he just won't stop talking!"
Translation: "He talks non-stop without much to say."

12. **Veg out**
Meaning: To relax completely or do nothing, often while watching TV.
Example: "Let's just veg out and watch a movie tonight."
Translation: "Let's just relax and watch a movie tonight."

13. **Vee**
Meaning: A shortcut for "very."
Example: "That's vee cool!"
Translation: "That's very cool!"

14. **Vocal**
Meaning: Expressing one's opinions openly and clearly.
Example: "She's very vocal about her opinions on politics."
Translation: "She expresses her opinions openly about politics."

15. **Vulnerable**
Meaning: In a weak or easily hurt position, often used when someone is open to emotional or physical harm.
Example: "He felt vulnerable after losing his job."
Translation: "He felt weak and exposed after losing his job."

16. **Vibe check**
Meaning: A way to assess or evaluate the mood or atmosphere of a situation or group of people.
Example: "Let's do a vibe check—are we all having fun?"
Translation: "Let's see how the mood is—are we all enjoying ourselves?"

17. Vex

Meaning: To annoy or disturb.
Example: "It really vexes me when people are late."
Translation: "It really annoys me when people are late."

18. Vouch

Meaning: To support or confirm something or someone's credibility.
Example: "I can vouch for her, she's great at her job."
Translation: "I can confirm she's great at her job."

19. Van

Meaning: Short for "vans," which refers to shoes or casual footwear.
Example: "I just bought a new pair of Vans."
Translation: "I just bought a new pair of shoes."

20. Vicarious

Meaning: Experiencing something indirectly, often through someone else's experience.
Example: "I live vicariously through my friend's adventures."
Translation: "I experience my friend's adventures through their stories."

W

1. **Wop-wops**
   Meaning: A remote or rural area, often far from the city.
   Example: "We're heading out to the wop-wops for the weekend."
   Translation: "We're heading out to the countryside for the weekend."

2. **Whānau**
   Meaning: A Māori word for family, often used to describe a close-knit group.
   Example: "We're having a big whānau dinner this weekend."
   Translation: "We're having a big family dinner this weekend."

3. **Wicked**
   Meaning: Something that is really cool, awesome, or impressive.
   Example: "That concert was wicked!"
   Translation: "That concert was amazing!"

4. **Woop woop**
   Meaning: A very remote or isolated place, similar to "wop-wops."
   Example: "They live all the way out in woop woop, it's a long drive!"
   Translation: "They live in a very remote place, it's a long drive!"

5. **Whinge**
   Meaning: To complain or whine about something.
   Example: "Stop whinging about the weather, it's not that bad."
   Translation: "Stop complaining about the weather, it's not that bad."

6. **Wobble**
   Meaning: To feel uncertain or unsteady, either physically or emotionally.
   Example: "I'm starting to wobble on this decision."
   Translation: "I'm starting to feel unsure about this decision."

7. **Waka**
   Meaning: A Māori term for a canoe or boat, but also used to refer to a vehicle or a means of transport.
   Example: "We're taking the waka to the beach tomorrow."
   Translation: "We're taking the car to the beach tomorrow."

8. **Whack**
   Meaning: To hit something or someone; also used to describe something strange or unusual.
   Example: "That movie was a bit whack, I didn't get it."
   Translation: "That movie was a bit strange, I didn't understand it."

9. **Wuss**
   Meaning: A person who is perceived as weak or afraid to do something.
   Example: "Don't be such a wuss, just jump in!"
   Translation: "Don't be such a coward, just jump in!"

10. **Wicked awesome**
    Meaning: A way of saying something is extremely impressive or amazing.
    Example: "That was wicked awesome, best day ever!"
    Translation: "That was incredibly awesome, best day ever!"

11. **Whacked out**
Meaning: To be very tired or exhausted, or sometimes used to describe someone who is acting strangely.
Example: "I'm whacked out after that long hike."
Translation: "I'm exhausted after that long hike."

12. **Waay**
Meaning: Used to emphasize something, similar to "so" or "really."
Example: "That was waay too much food!"
Translation: "That was really too much food!"

13. **Wheedle**
Meaning: To coax or persuade someone to do something, often in a subtle or insistent manner.
Example: "He tried to wheedle some money out of me for the concert."
Translation: "He tried to persuade me to give him some money for the concert."

14. **Wander**
Meaning: To walk aimlessly or without a particular direction.
Example: "I like to wander around the city when I'm free."
Translation: "I like to walk around the city without any particular plan when I'm free."

15. **Wheeler-dealer**
Meaning: A person who is good at negotiating or making deals, often in a sly or shrewd manner.
Example: "He's a real wheeler-dealer when it comes to buying and selling cars."

Translation: "He's very good at making deals when it comes to buying and selling cars."

16. **Work your arse off**
Meaning: To work very hard.
Example: "I've been working my arse off to get this project done on time."
Translation: "I've been working extremely hard to get this project done on time."

17. **Whacked**
Meaning: Extremely tired or worn out.
Example: "I'm feeling whacked after that workout!"
Translation: "I'm feeling exhausted after that workout!"

18. **Wanderlust**
Meaning: A strong desire or longing to travel.
Example: "She's got serious wanderlust after visiting Europe last summer."
Translation: "She has a strong desire to travel after visiting Europe last summer."

19. **Warming up**
Meaning: To become more comfortable or to engage in a more relaxed state.
Example: "Let's just start warming up before we get into the big meeting."
Translation: "Let's just get comfortable before we get into the big meeting."

20. **Whip out**
Meaning: To take something out quickly, often with sudden or dramatic effect.
Example: "He whipped out his phone to show me the pictures."
Translation: "He took out his phone quickly to show me the pictures."

X

1. X Factor

Meaning: A noteworthy special talent or quality that makes someone stand out.

Example: "She's got the X factor, I can see her going far in the competition."

Translation: "She has a special quality that makes her stand out; I can see her going far in the competition."

2. Xenial

Meaning: Relating to hospitality, especially the relationship between a host and guest.

Example: "They were very xenial, making sure we felt comfortable during our stay."

Translation: "They were very hospitable, making sure we felt comfortable during our stay."

3. Xmas

Meaning: An informal abbreviation for Christmas.

Example: "We're having a big family dinner for Xmas."

Translation: "We're having a big family dinner for Christmas."

4. Xenophobia

Meaning: A fear or dislike of people from other countries or cultures.

Example: "The rise in xenophobia has made the community less welcoming."

Translation: "The increase in fear of outsiders has made the community less welcoming."

5. X-rated

Meaning: Used to describe content that is

explicit or inappropriate for children, often referring to adult films.

Example: "That movie was X-rated, so we had to watch it in private."

Translation: "That movie was explicit, so we had to watch it privately."

6. **Xenial vibe**

Meaning: The feeling or atmosphere created by a warm and welcoming host.

Example: "The house had a real xenial vibe, everyone felt at home."

Translation: "The house had a really welcoming atmosphere, everyone felt at home."

7. **X-factor personality**

Meaning: Someone with an engaging or captivating personality that attracts attention.

Example: "That guy has an X-factor personality, everyone loves talking to him."

Translation: "That guy has a captivating personality, everyone enjoys talking to him."

8. **Xtreme**

Meaning: A shorthand for extreme, often used to describe intense activities or situations.

Example: "They're into xtreme sports like bungee jumping and skydiving."

Translation: "They're into extreme sports like bungee jumping and skydiving."

9. **X-cellent**

Meaning: A playful variation of "excellent," used to emphasize something as very good.

Example: "That was an x-cellent performance, you nailed it!"

Translation: "That was an excellent performance, you nailed it!"

10. **Xenon**
    Meaning: A rare element used metaphorically to refer to something rare or unusual.
    Example: "Her talent is like xenon, you don't come across it every day."
    Translation: "Her talent is rare, you don't come across it often."

11. **Xmas party**
    Meaning: A Christmas party, often used informally.
    Example: "We're hosting an Xmas party at our place this year."
    Translation: "We're hosting a Christmas party at our place this year."

12. **Xander**
    Meaning: A trendy or modern name sometimes used to refer to someone cool.
    Example: "Xander's always the life of the party."
    Translation: "Xander is always the most fun at the party."

13. **X-treme makeover**
    Meaning: A dramatic change or transformation, often used in reference to appearance or living space.
    Example: "They gave the house an x-treme makeover and it looks amazing!"
    Translation: "They completely renovated the house and it looks amazing!"

14. **Xperience**
    Meaning: A creative spelling of "experience," often used for emphasis or branding.
    Example: "The xperience at that concert was unforgettable."

Translation: "The experience at that concert was unforgettable."

15. **X-rayed**
Meaning: Used to describe something being thoroughly examined or analyzed.
Example: "The proposal was x-rayed by the team before the meeting."
Translation: "The proposal was thoroughly reviewed by the team before the meeting."

16. **Xclusive**
Meaning: A creative variation of "exclusive," often used for emphasis.
Example: "We're going to an xclusive event this weekend."
Translation: "We're going to an exclusive event this weekend."

17. **X-tra**
Meaning: An exaggerated version of "extra," used to describe someone or something that is over the top.
Example: "She's always x-tra with her outfits, but she pulls it off!"
Translation: "She's always over the top with her outfits, but she pulls it off!"

18. **Xotic**
Meaning: A playful variation of "exotic," used to describe something or someone unique or unusual.
Example: "She's wearing an xotic dress tonight."
Translation: "She's wearing an exotic dress tonight."

19. **Xpression**
Meaning: A playful variation of "expression," often used for emphasis in music or art.

Example: "His xpression of emotion through his art is incredible."
Translation: "His expression of emotion through his art is incredible."

20. **Xenial heart**

Meaning: A person with a kind, warm, and hospitable nature.

Example: "She has a xenial heart, always making everyone feel welcome."

Translation: "She has a warm and welcoming heart."

Y

1. **Yarn**
   Meaning: A long, often exaggerated story or tale.
   Example: "He was telling me a yarn about his adventures in Europe."
   Translation: "He was telling me a long story about his adventures in Europe."

2. **Yuck**
   Meaning: An expression of disgust or distaste.
   Example: "Yuck, this food tastes terrible!"
   Translation: "This food tastes terrible!"

3. **Yolo**
   Meaning: An acronym for "You Only Live Once," used to justify doing something adventurous or risky.
   Example: "I'm going skydiving tomorrow, yolo!"
   Translation: "I'm going skydiving tomorrow, because you only live once!"

4. **Yarn bombing**
   Meaning: The act of covering public objects like trees or statues with knitted or crocheted material.
   Example: "They did some yarn bombing around town for the art festival."
   Translation: "They covered public objects with knitted pieces around town for the art festival."

5. **Yapper**
   Meaning: Someone who talks too much, often in an annoying way.
   Example: "She's such a yapper, I can't get a word in!"

Translation: "She talks so much, I can't get a word in!"

6. **Yuck it up**
Meaning: To laugh or joke around a lot, often in a loud or exaggerated manner.
Example: "We were yucking it up during the game last night."
Translation: "We were laughing a lot during the game last night."

7. **Yobbo**
Meaning: A derogatory term for a person who is loud, rude, and uncouth, often associated with bad behavior.
Example: "That guy is such a yobbo, always causing trouble."
Translation: "That guy is rude and always causing trouble."

8. **Yeehaw**
Meaning: An exclamation of excitement or joy, often associated with country or cowboy culture.
Example: "Yeehaw, we won the game!"
Translation: "Hooray, we won the game!"

9. **Yowie**
Meaning: A mythical creature from Australian folklore, similar to Bigfoot.
Example: "They say a yowie lives in these woods."
Translation: "They say a mythical creature lives in these woods."

10. **Yuck factor**
Meaning: The level of disgust or unpleasantness associated with something.
Example: "That's a real yuck factor for me, I can't eat that!"

Translation: "That's really unpleasant for me, I can't eat that!"

11. **Yes man**
    Meaning: A person who always agrees with others, usually to gain favor or avoid conflict.
    Example: "He's just a yes man, always agreeing with the boss."
    Translation: "He's always agreeing with the boss to avoid conflict."

12. **Yarndance**
    Meaning: A type of energetic or spontaneous movement, often in a social setting.
    Example: "We all joined in on the yarndance at the party last night."
    Translation: "We all joined in on the fun dancing at the party last night."

13. **Yippee**
    Meaning: An exclamation of joy or excitement.
    Example: "Yippee, we're going to the beach!"
    Translation: "Hooray, we're going to the beach!"

14. **Yowza**
    Meaning: An exclamation of surprise or amazement.
    Example: "Yowza, that was one intense game!"
    Translation: "Wow, that was one intense game!"

15. **Yob**
    Meaning: A person who is uncultured or behaves in a crude, loud manner.
    Example: "Don't act like a yob, be respectful!"
    Translation: "Don't act rudely, be respectful!"

16. **Yakka**
    Meaning: Work or labor, especially hard or physical work.

Example: "We've been doing a lot of yakka to finish the project on time."
Translation: "We've been working hard to finish the project on time."

17. **Yum**

Meaning: A word used to express that something tastes delicious.
Example: "This cake is so yum!"
Translation: "This cake is so delicious!"

18. **You beaut**

Meaning: An expression of admiration or approval, often used in response to something impressive.
Example: "That's a you beaut car you've got there!"
Translation: "That's an amazing car you've got there!"

19. **Yoda**

Meaning: A wise person, often used to refer to someone who is seen as a mentor or guide.
Example: "He's our Yoda when it comes to coding."
Translation: "He's our wise mentor when it comes to coding."

20. **Ying-yang**

Meaning: A situation or person with two contrasting but complementary qualities.
Example: "Their personalities are like ying-yang, they balance each other out."
Translation: "Their personalities are very different but complement each other."

Z

1. **Zonked**
   Meaning: Extremely tired or exhausted.
   Example: "I'm totally zonked after that long hike!"
   Translation: "I'm completely exhausted after that long hike!"

2. **Zinger**
   Meaning: A witty or sharp remark, often humorous.
   Example: "He came out with a zinger that had everyone laughing."
   Translation: "He made a sharp, funny remark that had everyone laughing."

3. **Zero in**
   Meaning: To focus attention on something, to target.
   Example: "I'm going to zero in on finishing this report today."
   Translation: "I'm going to focus completely on finishing this report today."

4. **Zig-zag**
   Meaning: To move back and forth in a pattern, often used to describe movement or planning.
   Example: "We had to zig-zag through the crowd to get to the stage."
   Translation: "We had to move back and forth through the crowd to get to the stage."

5. **Zonk**
   Meaning: To hit or strike with force, or to fall asleep quickly due to exhaustion.
   Example: "He zonked out as soon as he hit the bed."

Translation: "He fell asleep instantly as soon as he lay on the bed."

6. **Zesty**
Meaning: Full of flavor or excitement, often used to describe food or personality.
Example: "This salsa has a zesty kick to it!"
Translation: "This salsa has a lot of flavor!"

7. **Zip it**
Meaning: A way of telling someone to be quiet or stop talking.
Example: "Could you zip it for a second, I need to concentrate."
Translation: "Could you be quiet for a second, I need to concentrate."

8. **Zipped up**
Meaning: To quickly and efficiently complete or finish something.
Example: "I've zipped up the presentation; we're ready to go!"
Translation: "I've quickly finished the presentation; we're ready to go!"

9. **Zoomer**
Meaning: A term used to refer to the younger generation, especially Gen Z.
Example: "The Zoomers are all into tech and social media."
Translation: "The younger generation is all into tech and social media."

10. **Zonked out**
Meaning: To fall asleep quickly, often due to exhaustion.
Example: "After the long drive, I zonked out as soon as I hit the pillow."
Translation: "I fell asleep instantly after the long drive."

11. **Zooted**

Meaning: A slang term meaning intoxicated or under the influence of drugs.

Example: "He was totally zooted at the party last night."

Translation: "He was really intoxicated at the party last night."

12. **Zap**

Meaning: To quickly and efficiently do something, or to destroy or eliminate.

Example: "I'll zap through these emails in no time."

Translation: "I'll quickly get through these emails."

13. **Zero tolerance**

Meaning: A policy or attitude of not accepting any level of a particular behavior.

Example: "Our school has a zero tolerance policy for bullying."

Translation: "Our school doesn't accept any bullying at all."

14. **Zany**

Meaning: Outlandish, eccentric, or playful in a silly way.

Example: "That's a zany idea, but I love it!"

Translation: "That's a silly idea, but I love it!"

15. **Zip line**

Meaning: An activity where you travel along a cable, often at a high speed, from one platform to another.

Example: "We're going zip lining through the forest this weekend!"

Translation: "We're going to travel along a cable in the forest this weekend!"

16. **Zipped**
Meaning: To move quickly or rapidly.
Example: "He zipped down the hill on his skateboard."
Translation: "He moved quickly down the hill on his skateboard."

17. **Zapped**
Meaning: To feel drained or tired, often after exertion.
Example: "I'm totally zapped after that workout!"
Translation: "I'm completely drained after that workout!"

18. **Zig**
Meaning: A sudden change in direction, often used in reference to a path or decision-making.
Example: "The trail zigged to the left, and we followed it."
Translation: "The trail turned sharply left, and we followed it."

19. **Zinger of a joke**
Meaning: A joke that is particularly sharp or clever.
Example: "That was a real zinger of a joke, everyone was cracking up."
Translation: "That was a really sharp and funny joke, everyone was laughing."

20. **Zoom**
Meaning: To move quickly, often used when referring to transportation or something happening at high speed.
Example: "We zoomed through the city to get to the concert on time."
Translation: "We moved quickly through the city to get to the concert on time.

Made in the USA
Las Vegas, NV
28 January 2025

17112145R00066